50 French Pastry Recipes for Home

By: Kelly Johnson

Table of Contents

- Croissants
- Pain au Chocolat
- Kouign-Amann
- Chaussons aux Pommes (Apple Turnovers)
- Palmier Cookies
- Paris-Brest
- Mille-Feuille (Napoleon)
- Tarte Tatin
- Clafoutis
- Crêpes Suzette
- Madeleines
- Financiers
- Canelés de Bordeaux
- Choux à la Crème (Cream Puffs)
- Profiteroles
- Éclairs au Chocolat
- Religieuse
- Saint-Honoré Cake
- Opera Cake
- Dacquoise
- Macarons
- Tarte au Citron (Lemon Tart)
- Tarte aux Fraises (Strawberry Tart)
- Galette des Rois
- Gâteau Basque
- Brioche à Tête
- Pain Suisse
- Far Breton
- Savarin au Rhum
- Baba au Rhum
- Flan Parisien
- Pithiviers
- Bûche de Noël
- Chaussons aux Framboises (Raspberry Turnovers)
- Praluline

- Tarte Tropézienne
- Croquembouche
- Gâteau Opéra
- Tarte aux Poires Bourdaloue
- Navettes de Marseille
- Pain d'Épices
- Fougasse Sucrée
- Merveilleux
- Gâteau de Savoie
- Gâteau Nantais
- Tarte au Chocolat
- Pain Perdu (French Toast)
- Riz au Lait
- Puits d'Amour
- Mont-Blanc

Croissants

Ingredients:

- 4 cups all-purpose flour
- 1/4 cup sugar
- 1 tbsp salt
- 1 tbsp instant yeast
- 1 1/4 cups whole milk, warm
- 1 cup unsalted butter, cold
- 1 egg (for egg wash)

Instructions:

1. Mix flour, sugar, salt, and yeast. Add warm milk and knead into dough.
2. Roll into a rectangle, wrap in plastic, and chill for 2 hours.
3. Roll out butter into a thin sheet and place on dough. Fold and roll out 3 times, chilling in between.
4. Roll dough, cut into triangles, and shape croissants. Let rise for 2 hours.
5. Brush with egg wash and bake at 375°F (190°C) for 20 minutes.

Pain au Chocolat

Ingredients:

- Croissant dough (see above)
- 1/2 cup dark chocolate batons
- 1 egg (for egg wash)

Instructions:

1. Roll croissant dough into a rectangle and cut into strips.
2. Place chocolate batons at the edge of each strip and roll into a log.
3. Let rise for 2 hours, brush with egg wash, and bake at 375°F (190°C) for 20 minutes.

Kouign-Amann

Ingredients:

- 2 cups all-purpose flour
- 1/2 tsp salt
- 1 tbsp sugar
- 1 tsp yeast
- 3/4 cup warm water
- 1 cup unsalted butter, cold
- 1/2 cup granulated sugar

Instructions:

1. Mix flour, salt, sugar, yeast, and warm water. Knead and chill for 1 hour.
2. Roll butter into a sheet and enclose in dough. Fold and roll out 3 times, chilling in between.
3. Roll out, sprinkle with sugar, fold, and roll again. Cut into squares and place in muffin tins.
4. Let rise for 2 hours, then bake at 375°F (190°C) for 25 minutes.

Chaussons aux Pommes (Apple Turnovers)

Ingredients:

- 1 sheet puff pastry
- 2 apples, peeled and diced
- 2 tbsp sugar
- 1/2 tsp cinnamon
- 1 tbsp butter
- 1 egg (for egg wash)

Instructions:

1. Cook apples, sugar, cinnamon, and butter until soft. Let cool.
2. Cut puff pastry into squares, place filling inside, and fold into triangles.
3. Brush with egg wash and bake at 375°F (190°C) for 20 minutes.

Palmier Cookies

Ingredients:

- 1 sheet puff pastry
- 1/2 cup granulated sugar

Instructions:

1. Sprinkle sugar on puff pastry and fold edges inward twice.
2. Chill, then slice into 1/2-inch pieces.
3. Bake at 400°F (200°C) for 15 minutes, flipping halfway.

Paris-Brest

Ingredients:

- **For Choux Pastry:**
    - 1/2 cup water
    - 1/2 cup milk
    - 1/2 cup butter
    - 1 cup flour
    - 4 eggs
- **For Praline Cream:**
    - 1 cup heavy cream
    - 1/2 cup praline paste
    - 1/4 cup powdered sugar

Instructions:

1. Heat water, milk, and butter. Stir in flour and cook until dough pulls away.
2. Cool slightly, then mix in eggs one by one. Pipe into a ring shape and bake at 375°F (190°C) for 30 minutes.
3. Whip cream with praline paste and sugar. Slice pastry, fill with cream, and dust with powdered sugar.

Mille-Feuille (Napoleon)

Ingredients:

- 1 sheet puff pastry
- **For Pastry Cream:**
    - 2 cups milk
    - 1/2 cup sugar
    - 3 egg yolks
    - 1/4 cup cornstarch
    - 1 tsp vanilla extract
- **For Glaze:**
    - 1/2 cup powdered sugar
    - 1 tbsp milk

Instructions:

1. Bake puff pastry at 375°F (190°C) for 15 minutes, then cool and cut into rectangles.
2. Heat milk, sugar, yolks, cornstarch, and vanilla until thickened. Cool.
3. Layer pastry and pastry cream. Top with glaze and chill before serving.

Tarte Tatin

Ingredients:

- 4 apples, peeled and sliced
- 1/2 cup sugar
- 1/4 cup butter
- 1 sheet puff pastry

Instructions:

1. Caramelize sugar and butter in an ovenproof skillet.
2. Arrange apples on top and place puff pastry over them.
3. Bake at 375°F (190°C) for 30 minutes. Invert onto a plate to serve.

Clafoutis

Ingredients:

- 2 cups cherries, pitted
- 3/4 cup sugar
- 1/2 cup flour
- 3 eggs
- 1 cup milk
- 1 tsp vanilla extract

Instructions:

1. Butter a baking dish and place cherries inside.
2. Mix sugar, flour, eggs, milk, and vanilla, then pour over cherries.
3. Bake at 375°F (190°C) for 35 minutes. Serve warm.

Crêpes Suzette

Ingredients:

- **For Crêpes:**
    - 1 cup all-purpose flour
    - 2 eggs
    - 1 1/4 cups milk
    - 1 tbsp sugar
    - 2 tbsp melted butter
- **For Orange Sauce:**
    - 1/2 cup fresh orange juice
    - Zest of 1 orange
    - 1/4 cup sugar
    - 2 tbsp butter
    - 2 tbsp Grand Marnier or Cointreau

Instructions:

1. Blend crêpe ingredients until smooth, then let rest for 30 minutes.
2. Cook thin crêpes in a buttered pan, flipping once.
3. Simmer orange juice, zest, sugar, and butter. Add Grand Marnier and flambé if desired.
4. Fold crêpes into quarters and coat with sauce before serving.

Madeleines

Ingredients:

- 1/2 cup butter, melted
- 2 eggs
- 1/2 cup sugar
- 3/4 cup flour
- 1/2 tsp baking powder
- 1 tsp vanilla extract

Instructions:

1. Beat eggs and sugar until fluffy. Fold in flour, baking powder, vanilla, and melted butter.
2. Chill batter for 1 hour.
3. Fill madeleine molds and bake at 375°F (190°C) for 10–12 minutes.

Financiers

Ingredients:

- 1/2 cup almond flour
- 1/2 cup powdered sugar
- 1/4 cup all-purpose flour
- 1/4 tsp baking powder
- 3 egg whites
- 1/4 cup browned butter

Instructions:

1. Mix almond flour, sugar, flour, and baking powder.
2. Whisk in egg whites, then browned butter.
3. Fill small molds and bake at 375°F (190°C) for 10–12 minutes.

Canelés de Bordeaux

Ingredients:

- 2 cups whole milk
- 2 tbsp butter
- 1 cup sugar
- 1 cup flour
- 2 eggs + 2 yolks
- 2 tbsp dark rum
- 1 tsp vanilla extract

Instructions:

1. Heat milk and butter until warm.
2. Whisk sugar, flour, eggs, rum, and vanilla, then add warm milk.
3. Chill batter overnight.
4. Fill canelé molds and bake at 450°F (230°C) for 10 minutes, then lower to 375°F (190°C) for 50 minutes.

Choux à la Crème (Cream Puffs)

Ingredients:

- **For Choux Pastry:**
    - 1/2 cup water
    - 1/2 cup milk
    - 1/2 cup butter
    - 1 cup flour
    - 4 eggs
- **For Filling:**
    - 1 cup heavy cream
    - 2 tbsp powdered sugar
    - 1 tsp vanilla extract

Instructions:

1. Heat water, milk, and butter. Stir in flour and cook until dough pulls away.
2. Cool slightly, then mix in eggs one by one.
3. Pipe onto a baking sheet and bake at 375°F (190°C) for 25 minutes.
4. Whip cream, sugar, and vanilla, then fill choux puffs.

Profiteroles

Ingredients:

- Choux pastry (see above)
- 1 cup vanilla ice cream
- 1/2 cup melted chocolate

Instructions:

1. Make choux pastry and bake as above.
2. Slice and fill with ice cream.
3. Drizzle with melted chocolate before serving.

Éclairs au Chocolat

Ingredients:

- Choux pastry (see above)
- **For Chocolate Pastry Cream:**
    - 2 cups milk
    - 1/2 cup sugar
    - 3 egg yolks
    - 1/4 cup cornstarch
    - 4 oz dark chocolate
- **For Chocolate Glaze:**
    - 4 oz dark chocolate
    - 2 tbsp butter

Instructions:

1. Make choux pastry and pipe into long strips. Bake at 375°F (190°C) for 25 minutes.
2. Heat milk, sugar, yolks, cornstarch, and chocolate until thick. Cool, then fill éclairs.
3. Melt chocolate and butter, then glaze éclairs.

Religieuse

Ingredients:

- Choux pastry (see above)
- Pastry cream (see éclairs)
- 1/2 cup chocolate ganache

Instructions:

1. Make choux pastry, piping small and large rounds. Bake and cool.
2. Fill both with pastry cream.
3. Stack small choux on top of the large one, securing with ganache.

Saint-Honoré Cake

Ingredients:

- **For Base:**
    - 1 sheet puff pastry
- **For Choux Pastry:**
    - 1/2 cup water
    - 1/2 cup milk
    - 1/2 cup butter
    - 1 cup flour
    - 4 eggs
- **For Filling:**
    - 1 cup pastry cream
    - 1 cup whipped cream
- **For Caramel:**
    - 1/2 cup sugar

Instructions:

1. Bake puff pastry at 375°F (190°C) for 15 minutes.
2. Make choux pastry, pipe small rounds, bake, and fill with pastry cream.
3. Melt sugar into caramel and dip filled choux in it.
4. Arrange caramelized choux around the puff pastry base.
5. Pipe whipped cream in the center.

Opera Cake

Ingredients:

- **For Almond Sponge Cake:**
    - 1/2 cup almond flour
    - 1/2 cup sugar
    - 1/2 cup all-purpose flour
    - 4 eggs
    - 2 egg whites
    - 2 tbsp melted butter
- **For Coffee Syrup:**
    - 1/2 cup strong coffee
    - 2 tbsp sugar
- **For Coffee Buttercream:**
    - 1/2 cup butter
    - 1 cup powdered sugar
    - 2 tbsp strong coffee
- **For Chocolate Ganache:**
    - 4 oz dark chocolate
    - 1/2 cup heavy cream

Instructions:

1. Beat eggs, sugar, almond flour, and flour. Fold in beaten egg whites and butter. Bake at 375°F (190°C) for 12 minutes.
2. Mix coffee and sugar to make syrup.
3. Whip butter, powdered sugar, and coffee for buttercream.
4. Heat chocolate and cream for ganache.
5. Assemble layers of almond sponge, coffee syrup, coffee buttercream, and ganache.
6. Chill before serving.

Dacquoise

Ingredients:

- 1 cup almond flour
- 1 cup powdered sugar
- 4 egg whites
- 1/4 cup granulated sugar

For Filling:

- 1 cup heavy cream
- 2 tbsp powdered sugar
- 1 tsp vanilla extract

Instructions:

1. Preheat oven to 325°F (165°C).
2. Sift almond flour and powdered sugar together.
3. Whisk egg whites until foamy, then gradually add granulated sugar and beat until stiff peaks form.
4. Fold in almond mixture gently.
5. Pipe into circles on a baking sheet and bake for 25 minutes.
6. Whip cream, powdered sugar, and vanilla.
7. Assemble by layering dacquoise discs with whipped cream.

Macarons

Ingredients:

- 1 cup almond flour
- 1 1/2 cups powdered sugar
- 3 egg whites
- 1/4 cup granulated sugar
- Food coloring (optional)

For Filling:

- 1/2 cup butter, softened
- 1 cup powdered sugar
- 1 tsp vanilla extract

Instructions:

1. Sift almond flour and powdered sugar together.
2. Whisk egg whites, gradually adding granulated sugar, until stiff peaks form.
3. Fold almond mixture into egg whites.
4. Pipe small rounds onto a baking sheet. Let rest for 30 minutes.
5. Bake at 300°F (150°C) for 15 minutes.
6. Beat butter, powdered sugar, and vanilla for filling.
7. Sandwich macarons with filling and chill before serving.

Tarte au Citron (Lemon Tart)

Ingredients:

- **For Crust:**
    - 1 1/4 cups flour
    - 1/2 cup butter
    - 1/4 cup sugar
    - 1 egg
- **For Lemon Curd:**
    - 3/4 cup lemon juice
    - 3 eggs
    - 3/4 cup sugar
    - 1/2 cup butter

Instructions:

1. Mix crust ingredients, roll out, and press into a tart pan. Bake at 350°F (175°C) for 15 minutes.
2. Heat lemon juice, eggs, sugar, and butter, stirring until thickened.
3. Pour into the crust and chill before serving.

Tarte aux Fraises (Strawberry Tart)

Ingredients:

- **For Crust:** (same as Tarte au Citron)
- **For Pastry Cream:**
    - 2 cups milk
    - 1/2 cup sugar
    - 3 egg yolks
    - 1/4 cup cornstarch
    - 1 tsp vanilla extract
- **Topping:**
    - 1 cup fresh strawberries

Instructions:

1. Bake crust as in Tarte au Citron.
2. Heat milk, sugar, yolks, cornstarch, and vanilla until thickened. Cool.
3. Fill crust with pastry cream and top with strawberries.

Galette des Rois

Ingredients:

- 2 sheets puff pastry
- **For Almond Cream Filling:**
    - 1/2 cup almond flour
    - 1/4 cup sugar
    - 1/4 cup butter
    - 1 egg
    - 1/2 tsp almond extract

Instructions:

1. Mix almond flour, sugar, butter, egg, and almond extract for filling.
2. Place filling on one puff pastry sheet, leaving edges clear.
3. Cover with second sheet, seal edges, and brush with egg wash.
4. Bake at 375°F (190°C) for 30 minutes.

Gâteau Basque

Ingredients:

- 1 1/2 cups flour
- 1/2 cup butter
- 1/2 cup sugar
- 2 eggs
- 1/2 cup pastry cream
- 1/2 cup cherry preserves

Instructions:

1. Mix flour, butter, sugar, and eggs into dough. Chill.
2. Divide dough, press half into a tart pan.
3. Spread pastry cream and cherry preserves over it.
4. Cover with remaining dough and bake at 350°F (175°C) for 35 minutes.

Brioche à Tête

Ingredients:

- 2 1/2 cups flour
- 1/4 cup sugar
- 1 tsp salt
- 1 packet yeast
- 3 eggs
- 1/2 cup butter, softened
- 1/4 cup milk

Instructions:

1. Mix flour, sugar, salt, and yeast.
2. Add eggs and milk, then knead in butter.
3. Let rise for 2 hours, then shape into small rounds with a small "head" on top.
4. Let rise for 1 more hour, then bake at 375°F (190°C) for 15 minutes.

Pain Suisse

Ingredients:

- **For Dough:**
    - 2 cups flour
    - 1/4 cup sugar
    - 1 tsp yeast
    - 1/2 cup milk
    - 1/4 cup butter
- **For Filling:**
    - 1/2 cup pastry cream
    - 1/2 cup chocolate chips

Instructions:

1. Mix dough ingredients and knead. Let rise for 2 hours.
2. Roll out dough, spread pastry cream and chocolate chips over half, then fold.
3. Cut into strips, let rise for 1 hour.
4. Bake at 375°F (190°C) for 15 minutes.

Far Breton

Ingredients:

- 2 cups whole milk
- 3/4 cup flour
- 1/2 cup sugar
- 3 eggs
- 1 tsp vanilla extract
- 1/2 cup prunes

Instructions:

1. Preheat oven to 375°F (190°C).
2. Blend milk, flour, sugar, eggs, and vanilla into a batter.
3. Pour into a buttered dish and add prunes.
4. Bake for 40 minutes until golden.

Savarin au Rhum

Ingredients:

- **For the Dough:**
    - 2 cups flour
    - 2 tbsp sugar
    - 1 tsp salt
    - 1 packet yeast
    - 3 eggs
    - 1/2 cup milk, warm
    - 1/4 cup butter, softened
- **For the Syrup:**
    - 1 cup water
    - 1/2 cup sugar
    - 1/4 cup dark rum
- **For Topping:**
    - 1 cup whipped cream
    - Fresh fruit (optional)

Instructions:

1. Mix flour, sugar, salt, yeast, eggs, and warm milk. Knead in butter and let rise for 1 hour.
2. Shape into a ring mold and let rise for 30 minutes.
3. Bake at 375°F (190°C) for 25 minutes.
4. Heat water and sugar for syrup, then add rum.
5. Soak the cake in syrup, then serve with whipped cream and fruit.

Baba au Rhum *(Similar to Savarin but with individual portions)*

Ingredients: *(Same as Savarin au Rhum, but portioned into small molds)*

Instructions:

1. Prepare and bake dough in small individual molds.
2. Make rum syrup and soak babas in it.
3. Serve with whipped cream and fruit.

Flan Parisien

Ingredients:

- **For the Crust:**
    - 1 sheet puff pastry
- **For the Custard Filling:**
    - 2 cups whole milk
    - 1 cup heavy cream
    - 3/4 cup sugar
    - 3 egg yolks
    - 1/4 cup cornstarch
    - 1 tsp vanilla extract

Instructions:

1. Preheat oven to 375°F (190°C).
2. Line a tart pan with puff pastry.
3. Heat milk, cream, and sugar. Whisk egg yolks, cornstarch, and vanilla, then temper with warm milk.
4. Cook until thickened, then pour into crust.
5. Bake for 45 minutes. Chill before serving.

Pithiviers

Ingredients:

- **For the Pastry:**
    - 2 sheets puff pastry
- **For the Almond Cream Filling:**
    - 1/2 cup almond flour
    - 1/4 cup sugar
    - 1/4 cup butter
    - 1 egg
    - 1/2 tsp almond extract

Instructions:

1. Mix almond flour, sugar, butter, egg, and almond extract.
2. Place filling on one puff pastry sheet, leaving edges clear. Cover with the second sheet and seal edges.
3. Brush with egg wash, score a pattern, and bake at 375°F (190°C) for 30 minutes.

Bûche de Noël (Yule Log Cake)

Ingredients:

- **For the Sponge Cake:**
    - 4 eggs
    - 1/2 cup sugar
    - 1/2 cup flour
    - 1/4 cup cocoa powder
- **For the Filling:**
    - 1 cup heavy cream
    - 2 tbsp powdered sugar
    - 1 tsp vanilla extract
- **For the Chocolate Ganache:**
    - 4 oz dark chocolate
    - 1/2 cup heavy cream

Instructions:

1. Beat eggs and sugar until fluffy. Fold in flour and cocoa powder. Spread on a baking sheet and bake at 375°F (190°C) for 12 minutes.
2. Roll cake in a towel while warm. Unroll and fill with whipped cream, then roll back up.
3. Pour ganache over and use a fork to create a bark texture.

Chaussons aux Framboises (Raspberry Turnovers)

Ingredients:

- 1 sheet puff pastry
- 1 cup fresh raspberries
- 2 tbsp sugar
- 1 tbsp lemon juice
- 1 egg (for egg wash)

Instructions:

1. Mash raspberries with sugar and lemon juice.
2. Cut puff pastry into squares, place filling inside, and fold into triangles.
3. Brush with egg wash and bake at 375°F (190°C) for 20 minutes.

Praluline *(Brioche with Praline Almonds)*

Ingredients:

- 2 1/2 cups flour
- 1/4 cup sugar
- 1 tsp salt
- 1 packet yeast
- 3 eggs
- 1/2 cup butter, softened
- 1 cup pink praline almonds (chopped caramelized almonds)

Instructions:

1. Mix flour, sugar, salt, and yeast. Add eggs and knead in butter. Let rise for 2 hours.
2. Fold in praline almonds and shape into a round loaf.
3. Let rise for 1 hour, then bake at 375°F (190°C) for 25 minutes.

Tarte Tropézienne *(Cream-Filled Brioche Cake)*

Ingredients:

- **For the Brioche:**
    - 2 1/2 cups flour
    - 1/4 cup sugar
    - 1 tsp yeast
    - 3 eggs
    - 1/2 cup butter
- **For the Cream Filling:**
    - 1 cup pastry cream
    - 1 cup whipped cream
    - 2 tbsp powdered sugar

Instructions:

1. Mix and knead brioche dough. Let rise for 2 hours. Shape into a round cake and let rise again.
2. Bake at 375°F (190°C) for 25 minutes. Cool.
3. Whip pastry cream and whipped cream together, then slice brioche and fill with cream.

Croquembouche *(Tower of Caramel-Coated Cream Puffs)*

Ingredients:

- **For the Choux Pastry:** *(see Choux à la Crème recipe above)*
- **For the Caramel:**
    - 1 cup sugar
    - 1/4 cup water

Instructions:

1. Make and bake small choux pastry rounds. Fill with pastry cream.
2. Heat sugar and water until caramelized.
3. Dip choux in caramel and stack into a cone shape, using caramel to hold them together.

Gâteau Opéra (Opera Cake)

Ingredients:

- **For Almond Sponge Cake:**
    - 1/2 cup almond flour
    - 1/2 cup sugar
    - 1/2 cup flour
    - 4 eggs
    - 2 egg whites
    - 2 tbsp melted butter
- **For Coffee Syrup:**
    - 1/2 cup strong coffee
    - 2 tbsp sugar
- **For Coffee Buttercream:**
    - 1/2 cup butter
    - 1 cup powdered sugar
    - 2 tbsp strong coffee
- **For Chocolate Ganache:**
    - 4 oz dark chocolate
    - 1/2 cup heavy cream

Instructions:

1. Beat eggs, sugar, almond flour, and flour. Fold in beaten egg whites and butter. Bake at 375°F (190°C) for 12 minutes.
2. Mix coffee and sugar for syrup.
3. Whip butter, powdered sugar, and coffee for buttercream.
4. Heat chocolate and cream for ganache.
5. Assemble layers of almond sponge, coffee syrup, coffee buttercream, and ganache.
6. Chill before serving.

Tarte aux Poires Bourdaloue (Pear and Almond Tart)

Ingredients:

- **For the Crust:**
    - 1 1/4 cups flour
    - 1/2 cup butter
    - 1/4 cup sugar
    - 1 egg
- **For the Almond Cream:**
    - 1/2 cup almond flour
    - 1/4 cup sugar
    - 1/4 cup butter
    - 1 egg
    - 1/2 tsp almond extract
- **For the Topping:**
    - 3 poached pears, halved and sliced
    - 2 tbsp apricot jam

Instructions:

1. Mix crust ingredients, roll out, and press into a tart pan. Chill for 30 minutes.
2. Preheat oven to 375°F (190°C).
3. Mix almond flour, sugar, butter, egg, and almond extract to make almond cream. Spread over crust.
4. Arrange pear slices on top.
5. Bake for 30 minutes. Brush with warm apricot jam before serving.

Navettes de Marseille (Orange Blossom Cookies)

Ingredients:

- 2 cups flour
- 1/2 cup sugar
- 1/4 cup butter, melted
- 1 egg
- 2 tbsp orange blossom water
- 1 tsp baking powder

Instructions:

1. Preheat oven to 350°F (175°C).
2. Mix flour, sugar, baking powder, melted butter, egg, and orange blossom water until smooth.
3. Shape into small boat-like cookies.
4. Bake for 15 minutes until lightly golden.

Pain d'Épices (French Spice Bread)

Ingredients:

- 2 cups rye flour
- 1/2 cup honey
- 1/2 cup brown sugar
- 3/4 cup milk
- 1 tsp baking soda
- 1 tsp cinnamon
- 1/2 tsp ground ginger
- 1/4 tsp nutmeg
- 1/4 tsp cloves

Instructions:

1. Preheat oven to 350°F (175°C).
2. Heat honey, sugar, and milk until warm.
3. Mix flour, baking soda, and spices. Add warm honey mixture.
4. Pour into a loaf pan and bake for 40 minutes.

Fougasse Sucrée (Sweet Fougasse)

Ingredients:

- 2 cups flour
- 1/4 cup sugar
- 1/2 tsp salt
- 1 tsp yeast
- 1/2 cup warm milk
- 1 egg
- 1/4 cup butter, softened
- 1 tbsp orange blossom water
- 2 tbsp pearl sugar

Instructions:

1. Mix flour, sugar, salt, and yeast. Add milk, egg, butter, and orange blossom water.
2. Knead dough and let rise for 2 hours.
3. Roll into a flat oval, cut slits, and let rise for another hour.
4. Brush with butter, sprinkle pearl sugar, and bake at 375°F (190°C) for 15 minutes.

Merveilleux (Chocolate-Coated Meringue with Whipped Cream)

Ingredients:

- **For the Meringues:**
    - 3 egg whites
    - 3/4 cup sugar
- **For the Filling:**
    - 1 cup heavy cream
    - 2 tbsp powdered sugar
    - 1 tsp vanilla extract
- **For the Coating:**
    - 4 oz dark chocolate, melted
    - 1/2 cup chocolate shavings

Instructions:

1. Preheat oven to 225°F (110°C). Beat egg whites until foamy, then gradually add sugar and beat until stiff peaks form.
2. Pipe small meringues onto a baking sheet and bake for 90 minutes. Let cool.
3. Whip cream, powdered sugar, and vanilla. Sandwich meringues with whipped cream.
4. Coat in melted chocolate and roll in chocolate shavings.

Gâteau de Savoie (Savoy Sponge Cake)

Ingredients:

- 4 eggs
- 3/4 cup sugar
- 3/4 cup flour
- 1/2 tsp baking powder
- 1 tsp vanilla extract
- Powdered sugar (for dusting)

Instructions:

1. Preheat oven to 350°F (175°C).
2. Separate eggs. Beat yolks with sugar until fluffy. Stir in vanilla.
3. Sift flour and baking powder, then fold into yolk mixture.
4. Beat egg whites until stiff peaks form, then fold into batter.
5. Pour into a buttered cake mold and bake for 30 minutes.
6. Cool and dust with powdered sugar before serving.

Gâteau Nantais (Rum-Soaked Almond Cake)

Ingredients:

- 1 cup almond flour
- 1/2 cup all-purpose flour
- 3/4 cup sugar
- 1/2 cup butter, softened
- 3 eggs
- 2 tbsp dark rum
- 1 tsp vanilla extract
- 1/2 tsp baking powder

For the Glaze:

- 1/2 cup powdered sugar
- 2 tbsp dark rum

Instructions:

1. Preheat oven to 350°F (175°C). Grease a cake pan.
2. Beat butter and sugar until creamy. Add eggs one at a time.
3. Mix in almond flour, all-purpose flour, baking powder, vanilla, and rum.
4. Pour into the pan and bake for 35–40 minutes.
5. Cool, then mix powdered sugar and rum for glaze. Spread over the cake before serving.

Tarte au Chocolat (French Chocolate Tart)

Ingredients:

- **For the Crust:**
    - 1 1/4 cups flour
    - 1/2 cup butter
    - 1/4 cup sugar
    - 1 egg
- **For the Filling:**
    - 7 oz dark chocolate
    - 3/4 cup heavy cream
    - 1/4 cup milk
    - 1 egg

Instructions:

1. Mix crust ingredients, roll out, and press into a tart pan. Chill for 30 minutes.
2. Bake at 375°F (190°C) for 15 minutes.
3. Heat cream and milk, then pour over chopped chocolate. Stir until smooth.
4. Whisk in the egg, then pour into the crust.
5. Bake at 325°F (160°C) for 12–15 minutes until set. Chill before serving.

Pain Perdu (French Toast)

Ingredients:

- 4 thick slices of brioche or French bread
- 2 eggs
- 1/2 cup milk
- 2 tbsp sugar
- 1 tsp vanilla extract
- 1/2 tsp cinnamon
- Butter for frying

Instructions:

1. Whisk eggs, milk, sugar, vanilla, and cinnamon in a shallow dish.
2. Dip each slice of bread in the mixture, soaking for a few seconds.
3. Melt butter in a pan over medium heat. Fry each slice for 2–3 minutes per side until golden brown.
4. Serve warm with powdered sugar, syrup, or fresh fruit.

Riz au Lait (French Rice Pudding)

Ingredients:

- 4 cups whole milk
- 1/2 cup short-grain rice
- 1/3 cup sugar
- 1 tsp vanilla extract
- 1/2 tsp cinnamon (optional)

Instructions:

1. Heat milk in a saucepan over low heat until steaming.
2. Add rice and stir occasionally, cooking for 30–40 minutes until creamy.
3. Stir in sugar, vanilla, and cinnamon if using.
4. Serve warm or chilled.

Puits d'Amour (Pastry Filled with Pastry Cream and Caramelized Sugar)

Ingredients:

- **For the Pastry:**
    - 1 sheet puff pastry
- **For the Pastry Cream:**
    - 2 cups milk
    - 1/2 cup sugar
    - 3 egg yolks
    - 1/4 cup cornstarch
    - 1 tsp vanilla extract
- **For the Caramel Glaze:**
    - 1/2 cup sugar
    - 2 tbsp water

Instructions:

1. Preheat oven to 375°F (190°C). Cut puff pastry into small circles and bake for 15 minutes.
2. Heat milk, sugar, yolks, cornstarch, and vanilla, whisking until thickened. Cool.
3. Cut off pastry tops and fill with pastry cream.
4. Heat sugar and water in a pan until golden caramel forms. Drizzle over pastries before serving.

Mont-Blanc (Chestnut Cream and Meringue Dessert)

Ingredients:

- **For the Meringue:**
    - 3 egg whites
    - 3/4 cup sugar
- **For the Chestnut Cream:**
    - 1 cup chestnut purée
    - 2 tbsp powdered sugar
    - 1/2 cup heavy cream
- **For Garnish:**
    - 1 cup whipped cream

Instructions:

1. Preheat oven to 225°F (110°C). Beat egg whites, adding sugar gradually, until stiff peaks form.
2. Pipe small meringue circles and bake for 90 minutes.
3. Mix chestnut purée with powdered sugar. Whip cream and fold into chestnut mixture.
4. Pipe chestnut cream over meringues in thin strands.
5. Top with whipped cream before serving.

www.ingramcontent.com/pod-product-compliance
Lightning Source LLC
LaVergne TN
LVHW081337060526
838201LV00055B/2705